Bridgnorth Nock and Wilson

The Extensive sale of Excellent modern furniture:

including a set of Capital mahogany dining tables; grand pianoforte, by

Erard; beautiful rich Brussels and Turkey carpets; hair & wool mattresses,

down beds; cellar of wines & spirits; library of boo

Bridgnorth Nock and Wilson

The Extensive sale of Excellent modern furniture:
*including a set of Capital mahogany dining tables; grand pianoforte, by Erard;
beautiful rich Brussels and Turkey carpets; hair & wool mattresses, down beds;
cellar of wines & spirits; library of boo*

ISBN/EAN: 9783744789905

Printed in Europe, USA, Canada, Australia, Japan

Cover: Foto ©Andreas Hilbeck / pixelio.de

More available books at **www.hansebooks.com**

EAST CASTLE STREET,

BRIDGNORTH.

CATALOGUE OF THE EXTENSIVE SALE OF EXCELLENT MODERN

FURNITURE

INCLUDING

A Set of Capital Mahogany Dining Tables,

Handsome Mahogany Sideboard, 12 well-made Mahogany Chairs, with Hair Seats ;
Mahogany Cheffioneer ; Beautiful Marble top Console Table ;
6 Solid Rosewood Chairs, with Horse Hair Seats, covered with Damask ; Pair of
Beautiful ROSEWOOD CHEFFIONEERS ; Noble Circular Loo Table ;
Carved Rosewood Sofa Table ; Fine-Toned & Costly

GRAND PIANOFORTE, BY ERARD,

LARGE HANDSOME CHIMNEY GLASSES,

Beautiful rich Brussels and Turkey Carpets,

Lofty Mahogany 4-POST and HALF-TESTER BEDSTEADS,
In admirably chosen patterns of Chintz & Moreen ;

HAIR & WOOL MATTRESSES, DOWN BEDS,

Mahogany Wardrobes ; Handsome Cabinet, fitted up with 12 Drawers ;

A SPLENDID MODEL OF JERUSALEM,

Mahogany and Painted Chests of Drawers ; Mahogany Wash Stands and Toilet Tables,
Handsome Swing Glasses, Cheval Ditto ; China Toilet Services,

CELLAR OF WINES & SPIRITS,

LIBRARY OF BOOKS,

OIL PAINTINGS & ENGRAVINGS,

Also a VALUABLE BAY CARRIAGE GELDING, 6 Years old ;

4-WHEEL CARRIAGE ; WELL-BUILT GIG;

HARNESS, SADDLES, BRIDLES, AND HORSE CLOTHING ;

2 RICKS OF HAY,

(TO GO OFF ;)

1200 Choice GREENHOUSE PLANTS,

GARDEN SEATS, CUCUMBER FRAMES, GARDEN TOOLS, &c.

MESSRS.

NOCK AND WILSON

Have the honor of announcing that they are instructed by the Executors of the late
Henry Vickers, Esq., to submit for Unreserved Competition, on

Monday, Tuesday, Wednesday, and Thursday,
the 23rd., 24th., 25th, & 26th. days of October, 1865,

The whole of the VALUABLE FURNITURE and other Items, all selected with much
taste, and without regard to expense.

The view day is appointed for Saturday preceding the Sale.   Admission by Catalogue only.

CONDITIONS OF SALE.

1. *That the highest bidder be the Purchaser, and if any dispute should arise between two or more Bidders, the Lot in dispute to be put up again and re-sold*

2. *The Biddings to be in the usual proportions, or at the discretion of the Auctioneers.*

3. *The lots to be taken by the Purchaser with all faults and errors (if any), and the purchase money to be paid at the fall of the hammer (if required), or at the close of each day's Sale.*

Lastly. Upon failure of complying with the above conditions, the Auctioneers shall be at liberty to re-sell the said Lots, either by public or private sale ; and the deficiency (if any there should be) by such second or re-sale, together with all charges attending the same, shall be made good by the defaulter at the present Sale.

NOCK AND WILSON,
AUCTIONEERS.

FIRST DAY'S SALE,

Monday, October 23, 1865,

COMMENCING AT 11 O'CLOCK.

Garden.

1 to 60 Twelve hundred pots of plants, consisting of Acacias, Azaleas, Camellias, Coronillas, Fuschias, Pelargoniums, Liliums, Oleanders, &c., in lots of 20 each
61 Nine hanging baskets, with plants
62 Two watering pans
63 Two pairs of steps
64 Six striking boxes
65 Three tubs for plants
66 Cucumber frame with glass light
67 Hand glass
68 Riddle and two kipes
69 Pair of garden shears & scythe
70 Two rakes and turf cutter
71 Stone garden roll with iron frame
72 Lot of ornamental garden wire
73 Two garden seats
74 Two ditto
75 Round table
76 Quantity of gutta percha tubing
77 Two baskets of seed potatoes
78 Brush and sulphur burner
79 Door scraper
80 Three flower pot stands
81 Quantity of flower pots, in lots
82 Wire lattice
83 Three thermometors
84 Six cucumber glasses
85 Three garden syringes
86 Two roller blinds
87 Sundries

Yard.

88 Riddle, coal hammer, and shovel
89 Wash and ash tub
90 Two sashes
91 Quantity of old cornice
92 Corn bin
93 Quantity of marble slabs
94 Quantity of old copper
95 Quantity of old iron
96 Lot of hampers
97 Pair of carriage shafts
98 Chaff box
99 Brass hat and umbrella stand
100 Sundries

Cellar.

101 Quarter barrel
102 Ditto
103 Ditto
104 Ditto
105 Ditto
106 Ditto
107 Ditto
108 Ditto
109 Ditto
110 Ditto

111 Mashing tub
112 Ditto
113 Mash rule, sieve, and ladder
114 Round tub
115 Ditto
116 Ditto
117 Ditto
118 Cooler
119 Tuupail and gaun
120 Several trams and stoopers
121 Quantity of glass bottles
122 Two oil cans
123 Bottle rack
124 Safe with wire front
125 Small ditto
126 Oak table

AFTERNOON SALE,

Commencing at 2 o'clock.

Entrance Hall.

127 Capital oak table
128 Four splendid carved oak chairs
129 Oak hat and umbrella stand
130 Barometer
131 Four mats
132 Door scraper
133 Piece of oil cloth, 15 ft., by 8 ft. 6 ins.

Dining Room.

134 Handsome fender & ashpan
135 Set of steel fire irons
136 Pair of lamps
137 Chimney ornaments
138 Noble chimney glass, in carved gilt frame, plate 5 ft. 6 ins. by 3 ft.
139 Twelve well-made mahogany chairs, with hair seats
140 Mahogany easy chair, with spring seat, upon castors
141 Ditto

142 Capital mahogany sideboard, 7 ft. 6 ins. by 2 ft. 4 ins., with two cellarets
143 Capital mahogany cheffioneer
144 Beautiful console table, marble top
145 Set of excellent mahogany dining tables, 14 ft. by 4 ft. 2 ins.
146 Two chair backs
147 Turkey carpet, 16 ft. by 13 ft. with rug to match
148 Beautiful four-light bronze gas pendant
149 Rosewood tea caddy
150 Quantity of oil cloth
151 Two crimson window curtains, with mahogany pole, gilt ends, massive rings, deep worsted fringe, and tassels, complete
152 Two mats
153 Two roller blinds

Glass and China.

154 Pair of decanters
155 Pair of claret ditto
156 Pair of quart ditto
157 Pair of ditto
158 Pair of ditto
159 Three cut pint decanters
160 Fourteen champagne glasses
161 Twelve ditto
162 Ten claret ditto
163 Twelve hock ditto
164 Twenty-eight wines
165 Seven ditto
166 Six odd ditto
167 Five ales
168 Three ditto
169 Twelve tumblers
170 Sixteen finger glasses
171 Ten blue ditto
172 Four liqueur glasses
173 Four hyacinth ditto
174 Six cut salts

175 Four handsome cut salts
176 Four jelly and five custard cups
177 Two cut dishes
178 Six water crofts
179 Three glass dishes
180 Three plates
181 Large dish
182 Butter cup and stand
183 Pickle stand
184 Three small stands
185 Two jugs
186 Two ditto
187 Eleven wine coolers
188 Glass jug
189 Sundry odd glass
190 Two large water bottles
191 Breakfast and tea service, 53 pieces

192 Beautiful tea service, containing 11 coffee cups, 11 tea cups, 12 saucers, 2 bread and butter plates, sugar basin and cream jug, slop basin, butter cup stand and cover, and teapot and stand
193 Blue & white dinner service
194 Odd ditto
195 Green dessert service, 15 pieces
196 White breakfast service, 46 pieces
197 Earthen wine cooler
198 Quantity of lamp glasses.
199 Sundries
200 Ditto
201 Ditto

END OF FIRST DAY'S SALE.

Books.

1 Dr. Jebb's Sermons and 4 other vols. of Sermons
2 Biblia Sacra, small 8vo., old calf. *Lug.* 1567, and 18 others.
3 Salmon's Geographical and Historical Grammar, 8vo., and 10 others
4 A Million of Facts by Sir Richard Phillips—Bailey's English Dictionary, and 8 others
5 Mill's Reply to Howitt on Priestcraft, and 4 others
6 White's Farriery, 3 vols., and 9 others
7 Walker's Gazetteer, 8vo. — Mawe's Gardener's Calendar, and 4 others
8 Sir Thomas Smith on the Commonwealth, 8vo., old calf. *London*, 1609, and 4 others
9 Falck-Lebahn's Practice of German, and several others
10 Musæ Cantabrigienses, 8vo., and 8 others
11 Scott's Lady of the Lake and Lord of the Isles, 2 vols., 8 vo.—Young's Night Thoughts, 8vo. and 3 others
12 Smollett's History of England, 10 vols, 8vo.— Martin's Correspondence, 4 vols., 8vo., half calf, *London*, 1759-64
13 Memoirs of Major General Burn, 2 vols,—Hartley's Researches in Greece, and 5 others
14 Goldsmith's Miscellaneous Works, 8vo--Zimmerman on Solitude, 2 vols., and 4 others
15 Life of Archbishop Laud—Sacred History, 2 vols., and 4 others
16 Fox's Christian Martyrdom, 8vo., and 6 others
17 Cruchley's Map of England and Wales, mounted on canvass, folded, and several books
18 Lindsay's Sermons 8vo., and several others

19 Badham's Treatise on the Esculent Funguses of
England, 8vo.—Hoare on the Grape Vine, 8vo.—
Forbes' Hortus Woburnensis 8vo., and 5 others
20 Malcolm's Londinium Redivivum, 4 vols., 4to, calf.
London, 1802
21 Buffon's Natural History, 9 vols., 8vo., calf,
London, 1791
22 The Spectator, 8 vols., 8vo., calf, *London* 1724
23 Hume's History of England, 8 vols., 8vo., grained
calf, *London* 1822
24 Robertson's Works, 10 vols., 8vo., grained calf,
London 1821
25 Chambers' Cyclopœdia of English Literature, 2 vols.
8vo.—Morrel's Philosophy and Science, 8vo.
26 O'Meara's Voice from St. Helena, 2 vols., 8vo.—
Count Montholon's History of the Captivity of
Napoleon, 2 vols., 8vo.
27 Literary Gazette, 1825 to 1829—Literary Chronicle,
1826 to 1828—Athenæum, 1828 to 1829—Court
Journal, 1829, 10 vols., 4to., half calf
28 Gibbon's Decline and Fall of the Roman Empire,
12 vols., 8vo., half calf, gilt. *London*, 1813
29 Blair's Sermons, 4 vols., 8vo., calf. *London*, 1791.
Gisborne's Survey of the Christian Religion,
8vo, calf
30 Owen and Blakeway's History of Shrewsbury,
2 vols., 4to., half calf, gilt. *London*, 1825
31 Memoirs of Sophia Dorothea, Consort of George I.,
2 vols., 8vo.—Letters of Mary Queen of Scots,
2 vols., 8vo.
32 Malcolm's Anecdotes of the Manners and Customs
of London, 5 vols., 8vo., calf. *London*, 1811—
Melmoth's Cicero, 3 vols., 8vo., calf. *Lon.*, 1799
33 Horne's Discourses, 3 vols., 8vo., calf. *London*,
1824—Fisk's Pastor's Memorial of the Holy
Land, 8vo.—Memoir of Rev. W. Wilkinson, 8vo.
34 Hawker's Commentary on the Bible, 9 vols., 8vo.,
grained calf. *London*, 1808
35 Mysteries of Paris, by Eugene Sue, 3 vols., large
8vo., illustrated. *London*, 1844 — Windsor
Castle, by Harrison Ainsworth, 8vo.
36 Smith's Wealth of Nations, 8vo.—De Lolme on the
English Constitution, 8vo., calf, gilt, & 2 others
37 Todd's Johnson's Dictionary, 4 vols., 4to., calf.
London, 1818
38 Bagster's English Hexapla, large 4to. *Lon.*, 1841

39 D'Oyley and Mant's Bible, 4to., with plates, 17 parts, complete, bds. *Oxford*, 1817 ... 7 6

40 Hugh Kelly's Works, 4to., *London*, 1778—Mickle's Poems, 4to.—Poetry of the Anti-Jacobin, 4to. ... 3 0

41 Gouldman's English Latin and Latin English Dictionary, small 4to. — Dr. Adam Littleton's English Latin and Latin English Dictionary, small 4to. ... 2 6

42 Novum Testamentum Græco-Latinum, vol. 1, fo. Basileæ, 1519—Biblia Septuaginta Interpretum, small 4to., vellum. *Londini*, 1653, and another ... 1 0 0

43 Catulli Tibulli et Propertii Opera—Publii Terentii afri Comœdiæ, 2 vols., 4to., red morocco, gilt edges. *Birmingham*, 1772 ... 1 5 0

44 Burnett's History of his own Time, 2 vols., fo., old calf. *London*, 1724

45 Cottage Gardener, vols. 14 to 25, and Horticultural Journal, vols. 1 to 7, cloth, and odd numbers of vol. 8 ... 1 16 0

46 Gurwood's Dispatches of the Duke of Wellington, 12 vols. and Index, 8vo., bds. *London*, 1834 ... 3 10 0

47 Colonel Napier's History of the Peninsular War, 6 vols., 8vo., bds. *London*, 1835 ... 3 5 0

48 The Percy Anecdotes, 20 vols , 24mo., calf, gilt. *London*, 1823 ... 2 2 0

49 Œuvres de Moliere, 8 vols., 12mo., grained calf. *Paris*, 1805 ... 10 0

50 Paley's Works, 8 vols., half calf, gilt. *Lon.*, 1814 ... 13 0

51 Christian Lady's Magazine, vols. 13 to 23, half calf, gilt, and odd numbers ... 16 0

52 Byron's Works, 10 vols., 12mo., calf gilt. *Lon.*, 1817 ... 17 0

53 Memoirs of Lady Hester Stanhope, 3 vols., 8vo. *London*, 1845—Sketches and Extracts from the Journal of Madame la Vicomtesse de Satge St. Jean, 8vo. *London*, 1843 ... 5 6

54 Shades of Character, 2 vols., half calf—Lobb's Contemplative Philosophy, 2 vols., grained calf ... 2 6

55 Scott's Rokeby, 8vo., half calf—Poems of Lady Flora Hastings—Poems by L. E. L., 2 vols. ... 14 0

56 The Royal Exile, 8vo., half calf. *London*, 1822, and 4 others

57 Salopia Antiqua, by Rev. C. H. Hartshorne, 8vo.— Antiquities of Bridgnorth, by Rev. G. Bellett ... 1 1 0

58 Francatelli's Cook's Guide, and 4 others ... 6 6

59 Camden's Britannia, fo., old calf. *London*, 1695, and another ... 7 0

60 Elegant Extracts in Verse, 8vo., calf —- Elegant
    Epistles, 8vo., calf—History of Rome, 3 vols.,
    8vo., half calf, and another

61 Botfield's Notes on the Cathedral Libraries of
    England, 8vo. *London*, 1849—Burke's Visitation
    of the Seats and Arms of the Noblemen and
    Gentlemen of Great Britain, 8vo. *London*, 1853

62 Stackhouse's History of the Bible, 2 vols., fo., old
    calf. *London*, 1742

63 Maitland's History of London, 2 vols., fo., old calf.
    London, 1772

64 Burnet's History of his own time, 2 vols., fo., old
    calf. *London*, 1724—Hooker's Works, small
    fo., old calf. *London*, 1636

~~65 Holy Bible, with Corbould's plates, large 4to.~~
    ~~handsomely bound. *London*, 1795~~

66 Strickland's Lives of the Queens of England, vols.
    1 to 8, *London*, 1841-45—Diary and Letters
    of Madame D'Arblay, vols. 1 to 5. *London* 1842

67 The Rogue, or the Life of Guzman de Alfarache,
    small fo., old calf. *London*, 1623 ·— Reed's
    Shakspeare, 12 vols. 12mo., calf, gilt. *London*,
    1809. (Vol. 10 wanting)

68 Schiller's Werke, large 8vo., half calf—*Stuttgart*,
    1840—Italian French and French Italian Dic-
    tionary, small 4to. 1686

69 Visit of the Prince Regent, Emperor of Russia, and
    King of Prussia, to the Corporation of London,
    in June 1814, fo., bds.—Thomson's Retreats,
    4to., bds. *London*, 1827—Pindar's Odes, 4to.,
    bds. *London*, 1792

70 Hume's England, 9 vols., 24mo., bds. *London*,
    1811, and 4 odd books

71 Bell's British Theatre, vols. 4 to 11, 13 and 18 to 20,
    and 22, 18mo., bds. *London*, 1797, and 6 odd
    books

72 Wonderful Museum, 6 vols., 8vo., half bound—
    Bingley's Animal Biography, 3 vols., half bound

73 Gifford's Life of Buonaparte, 2 vols., half bound—
    History of the French Revolution, 2 vols., 8vo.,
    calf—Bingley's Animal Biography, 3 vols., 8vo.,
    red roan, gilt

74 Finden's Views of Ports, Harbours, &c., of Great
    Britain, parts 1 to 19—France Illustrated, parts
    1 to 19—Hogarth's Works, in parts. (A few
    parts missing.)

		£	s
75	Quantity of odd Numbers of Court Magazine, Ainsworth's Magazine—Sharpe's Magazine, Edinburgh Tales, &c.	3	6
76	Annual Register, vols. 1 to 17, 19 to 28, 30 to 33, 35 to 45, calf	6	6
77	Scott's Novels, 25 vols., 1862-63, paper covers	19	0
78	Cornhill Magazine, vols 1 to 10, cloth, and January to September in numbers and odd numbers	1 14	0
79	Holy Bible, with Scott's Commentary, profusely illustrated, 1 thick vol., 4to., handsomely bound in morocco, gilt edges	1 11	0
80	Elegant Extracts, Prose 2 vols., Verse 2 vols, Epistles 2 vols., 8vo., half russia	11	0
81	History of the Russian War, 3 vols , large 8vo., half morocco, gilt edges	14	0
82	Holy Bible, 8vo., and several others ————	1	6
83	Bannister's Survey of the Holy Land, 8vo. *Bath*, 1844—The Novitiate, by Heinmetz, post 8vo., and 2 others	4	6
84	Layard's Nineveh, crown 8vo.—Abercrombie on the Intellectual Powers, post 8vo., and 3 others	7	0
85	Eliza Cook's Journal, vols. 1 and 2, and 3 others	4	6
86	Lodge's Peerage, 1847—Burke's Peerage, 1851, &c.	4	6
87	Half Hours with the Best Authors, 2 vols., 8vo.—Travelling Journal of Madame la Vicomtesse de Satge St. Jean, 8vo.—Byron's Poetical Works	11	0
88	Shakspeare's Dramatic Works, Diamond Edition—The Golden Violet and other Poems, by L. E. L., and 8 others	3	6
89	The King's Highway, and 9 other Novels, by G. P. R. James	5	0
90	"What will he do with it," 2 vols., and 3 other Novels by Bulwer Lytton—"The Spy," and 5 other Novels by J. F. Cooper	7	0
91	Amy Herbert — Katherine Ashton — The Earl's Daughter, 3 vols., and 4 others	8	0
92	Falck-Labahn's Self Instructor in German, and 6 other German and Italian Books	5	6
93	Meadows' French English and English French Pronouncing Dictionary, and 6 other French books	6	0
94	Arrowsmith's School Atlas of Ancient Geography, and 9 other School Books	5	6
95	Illustrated London News, 1846, 2 vols.—1863, 2 vols., cloth	7	0
96	Good Words, parts 1864, and odd parts—Sunday at Home, parts, 1864, and odd parts, &c.	4	0

Rath

Hermann
Rath
Wild

97 Tom Jones, 2 vols., half calf, and 11 others
98 Crivelli's Art of Singing, and odd Music
99 Bishop's Operas, 6 vols., half bound
100 Vocal Compositions of Mozart—British Melodies—
    Welsh Melodies, 3 vols., half bound
101 Vocal Music, 4 vols., half bound
102 Odd Music
103 Music Folios, Port Folio and Drawings, and Pho-
    tographic Album
104 The Law Journal from its commencement in 1822
    to December 1862, half law calf, with parts
    unbound up to the present time ; and Analytical
    Digests, boards
105 Cunningham's Law Dictionary, 2 vols., fo. *London*,
    1765, and several other Law Books
106 Cruise's Digest of the Laws of England, 6 vols.,
    8vo., law calf, and several others
107 Durnford's Reports, 8 vols., 8vo.—East's Reports,
    vols. 1 to 16, 8vo., and 4 other vols. of Reports,
    8vo., law calf
108 Vesey's Reports, vols. 1 to 13, law calf, and several
    other vols. of Reports
109 Saunder's Reports, 2 vols., 8vo., law calf, and
    several others
110 Barnewall and Cresswell's, and Adolphus & Ellis's
    Reports, several vols. in parts
111 Bridgman's Digested Index, 3 vols., 8vo., law calf,
    and several others
112 Bacon's Abridgement of the Law, 7 vols., 8vo.,
    law calf, and 3 others
113 Blackstone's Commentaries, 4 vols., 8vo., law calf.
    —Burn's Justice of the Peace, 5 vols., 8vo., law
    calf, and Supplement—Burn's Ecclesiastical Law
    4 vols., boards
114 Petersdorff's Common Law Reports, vols. 1 to 15,
    8vo., boards
115 Selwyn's Law of Nisi Prius, 2 vols., 8vo., law calf,
    and 4 others
116 Evans' Collection of Statutes, 8 vols , 8vo., law
    calf, and a few others
117 Cruise's Digest of the Law of England, by White,
    7 vols., large 8vo., boards, and a few others
118 The Statutes, I. to VI. Victoria, 5 vols., cloth,
    and several others
119 Quantity of other Books in lots
120 Quantity of Waste Paper and odd Books, in lots

121 Greenwood's Map of the County of Salop on canvass and rollers
122 Ditto
123 Pair of large Globes, by Bardin, in good condition, upon pedestals
124 Quantity of Minerals and Fossils

Oil Paintings, Engravings, &c.

125 Engraved Portrait in neat gilt frame—Engraved Portrait, coloured, in neat gilt frame
126 Two Pencil Drawings, in neat gilt frames
127 A fine Lithograph, "Canterbury Cathedral," in handsome gilt frame
128 Pair of coloured Engravings—Napoleon, "Au Pont D'Arcole"—Napoleon, "A Sainte Helene," in black frames
129 Three Coloured Engravings, neatly framed
130 Coloured Engraving, "The Fortune Teller," in gilt frame, and an Engraving in maple frame
131 Coloured Engraving, "The Duke of Wellington," in black frame, and two others
132 Coloured Engraving, "The Deserted Village, in black frame, and another in gilt frame
133 Three Studies—Heads
134 Water Colour Drawing, in neat gilt frame
135 Water Colour Drawing, "Evening," in neat gilt frame
136 Three gilt frames
137 Pair of small Oil Paintings, in neat gilt frames
138 Valuable Oil Painting, "The Violin Player," in handsome gilt frame
139 Valuable Oil Painting, "An Interior," in handsome gilt frame
140 Large Oil Painting—Sea Piece—in very handsome gilt frame
141 Ditto—A Landscape—in very handsome & massive gilt frame
142 Ditto—A Waterfall—in very handsome & massive gilt frame
143 Oil Painting, "The Smugglers," in handsome gilt frame
144 Oil Painting—A Landscape—in very handsome gilt frame
145 Engraving, "The Wellington Banquet," a very fine impression, handsomely framed and glazed, with key

Vild
Chilworth
Blackmoore

Bolurstol

Bratte
Ellison
Mrs Olinge

Millington
Vinow
Shinfield
~~Bordley~~
~~Shinsfield~~
Dennys
Wyley

Summers
C. Cooper
Bratte
Dutton
Davis
Summers

Mr Bosthwell

[Illegible handwritten notes]

Warden.
Sutton.

Sutton
Cole Sutton

Sutton
Do Do

Allison 44/-

Warrds 48/-
Do 54/-

Bombay 50/-

146 Engraving, "Night," after Landseer, Proof impression, in very handsome gilt frame, & glazed

147 Ditto, "Morning," after Landseer, framed to match

148 Ditto, "Charles XII. in the Studio of Titian," in neat gilt frame, and glazed

149 Ditto, "Oliver Cromwell and his Private Secretary John Milton," a fine impression, in handsome gilt frame, and glazed

150 Ditto, "Return from Deer Stalking," in neat gilt frame, and glazed

151 Pair of small Engravings, in neat gilt frames, and glazed, "The Newfoundland," and "The Retriever"

152 Three Engravings—"Shoeing," "A Scene in the Highlands," and another, in very neat gilt frames, and glazed

153 Small Drawing in Water Colours, "View of Quatford from the Churchyard," in neat gilt frame, and glazed

154 Mezzotint Engraving, "Portrait of Nelson," in neat gilt frame, glazed

155 Ditto, "Lady Elizabeth Grey emploring Edward IV. for the restitution of her husband's lands," in gilt frame, and glazed

156 Two Engravings, in maple frames, glazed

157 Four Proof Prints, in neat maple frames, glazed

158 Three small Coloured Engravings, in neat maple frames, glazed

159 Three Coloured Engravings, framed and glazed

160 Three Engraved Portraits, in neat frames

Wine Cellar.

Bin No. 1.

161 Two dozen of old sherry

162 Two dozen ditto

163 Two dozen ditto

164 Two dozen ditto, more or less

Bin No. 4.

165 Three dozen bottles of sherry

Bin No. 9.

166 Three dozen fine old sherry

Bin No. 3.

167 Two dozen old port, vintage not known

168 Two dozen old port, vintage not known

169 Two dozen ditto

170 Two dozen ditto, more or less

Bin No. 8.

171 Two dozen old port

172 Two dozen ditto, more or less

Bin No. 20 & 33.

173 Two dozen old port

174 Two dozen ditto, more or less

Bin No. 32.

175 Eighteen bottles of old port

Bin No. **1.**

:en bottles of claret

Bin No. **25.**

ittles of claret, and 10
les of French wine

Bin No. **19.**

ozen of claret

Bin No. **28.**

lozen of champagne

Bin No. **1.**

a bottles moussirender
elle

Bin, No. **26.**

dozen of sparkling
selle

Bin, No. **15.**

:en bottles of Moselle

Bin, No. **27.**

:en bottles of sparkling
:k

ozen of Still Hock in

£2-8 2 6 *Bin, No.* **30.**

185 Fourteen bottles of Beaujolais

186 Twelve ditto ditto in box

£1-16 *Bin 24 and* **29.**

187 Thirty bottles of light wines

188 Several dozens of wines,
(various), particulars of
which will be given at the
time of sale

189 Several dozens of home-made
wines

Spirits.

190 Six bottles of fine old Scotch
Whisky

191 Six ditto ditto

192 Six ditto ditto

193 Six bottles of Old Tom

194 Six ditto ditto

195 Seven ditto ditto

196 Nine bottles of fine old
French brandy

---

197 Several dozens of bottled ale

198 Ditto   ditto   of cider

199 Ditto   ditto   of perry

END OF SECOND DAY'S SALE.

-5 Oakw
-19 Varaw

Bonne-
te
War

Wer

Gum

.

Haa

THIRD DAY'S SALE,

Wednesday, Oct. 25, 1865,

COMMENCING AT 11 O'CLOCK.

Butler's Pantry.

£	s		
16	0	1	Cloth press *Walford*
4	0	2	Mahogany butler's tray and stand *Kirtland*
12	0	3	Ditto supper tray *Brown*
2	0	4	Small looking glass
2	6	5	Pair of chamber candlesticks
8	0	6	Pair of ditto *Warren*
		7	Bronze tea urn and stand
1	6	8	Ditto
5	0	9	Two waiters and plate basket
		10	Papier tray and mahogany knife tray *Oliver*
3	6	11	Bread tray and knife
1	6	12	Two hot water bottles *Summer*
4	3	13	Four hot water cans *Batt*
5	0	14	Percolator *Hopwood*
1	0	15	Three japan knife and bread trays *Simms*
10	0	16	Twelve table knives & forks
4	6	17	Five ditto ditto *Kirtland*
12	6	18	Four pairs of carvers *Simms*
12	6	19	Twelve dessert knives & forks *Brown*
		20	Odd ditto
6	0	21	Mahogany supper tray, fitted with dishes *Shepheard*
1	0	22	Odd dessert service *Warren*
9	6	23	Two large cups and one jug
2	1	24	Broth basin, cork screw, and sundries *Shepheard*

Housemaid's Closet.

£	s		
4	9	25	Quantity of black lead and other brushes *Owen*

26 Leg rest
27 Boot jack
28 Lot of worsted fring
29 Ditto cornice
30 Church cushions
31 Sundries

Morning Roo

32 Cast-iron fender
33 Set of fire irons
34 Chimney ornament:
35 Rosewood tea cadd
36 Bronze inkstand
37 Music stand and ta
38 Chimney glass, in 3 ft. by 20 in.
39 Six mahogany chai
40 Capital mahogany hair mattress, &
41 Mahogany sofa tabl
42 Mahogany table up leather top
43 Ditto secretaire, w case & glass fol
44 Handsome table lar
45 Ditto *Musgrove*
46 Pier glass, 3 ft. 9 in
47 Drugget, 15 ft. by
48 Crimson window cu rod
49 Roller blind

Middle Roo

50 Capital fender
51 Set of fire irons

res *Langford*
rnaments *[illegible]*
cheffioneer *Simmons*
kcase, glass front,
6 ft. 8 ins. *Botte*
ble, marble top *[illegible]*
any chairs *Austi*
fit room *Batte*
ter slides
es of oilcloth *Hawkins*
oreen window cur-
ith gilt pole
ase *[illegible]*
ols *A C*

OON SALE,

ng at 2 o'clock.

Landing.

lsome pier table,
arble slab *Mock*
es of new Brussels
11 yards *[illegible]*
t to match, 8 yards *[illegible]*
rass stair rods *hurrell*
[illegible]
Do

oreen window cur-
ith gilt pole, rings,
ks *Warren*
d
lcloth *Button*

. Articles.

dlesticks *Warren*
o
nch ditto
o
mber ditto
et *Turnbull*
n *Simmons*

ng Room.

steel fender *Warren*
eel fire irons and
[illegible]

81 China and other
naments
82 Very handsome
piece, with g
83 Large handson
glass, in carv
plate 3 ft. 9
11 ins.
84 Two figures witl
85 Flowers with dit
86 Pair of glass lust
87 Beautiful rosewo
marble slab,
back, in rich
88 Ditto ditto
89 Pair of footstool
90 Grand piano-for
91 Mahogany music
92 Mahogany cante
93 Harp
94 Beautiful rosewc
95 Elegant carved r
table
96 Capital rosewood
seat, covered
with extra cl
97 Six rosewood
hair seats,
damask, witl
covers
98 Rosewood arm
seat, extra cl
99 Neat rosewood
seat, covered
2 extra chin
100 Handsome glas
101 Ditto
102 Beautiful torto
box, neatly i
pearl
103 Papier mache t
104 Two ditto chai
105 Green moreen
dow curtains
some cornice
fringe, band

106 Set of muslin curtains *Westm*
107 Two footstools, needlework covers
108 Rich Brussels carpet, nearly new, 17 ft. by 16 ft. *Hancock*
109 Rug to match *Do*
110 Rug and piece of carpet to match *Renfrew*
111 Mat and piece of oil cloth
112 Three roller blinds

Best Chamber.

113 Set of handsome fluted 4-post bedsteads, with rich chintz furniture, lined with cambric
114 Mahogany cornice, with straw mattress
115 Large wool mattress
116 Capital down bed, bolster, and 2 pillows *Hughenhall*
117 Pair of large sized blankets
118 Under ditto *West*
119 Large marseilles quilt *Square*
120 Handsome brass fender *Vernall*
121 Set of fire irons *Warner*
122 Chimney ornaments *Brewster*
123 Chair bedstead, with hair cushions and chintz cover
124 Mahogany biddette *Brown*
125 Large mahogany wash stand with 2 drawers *Wagner*
126 White foot pan *Hall*
127 Handsome toilet service, 18 pieces *Green*
128 Water bottle and goblet *Miller*
129 Pair of mahogany fire screen poles *Cartwright*
130 Book shelf *Brown*
131 Mahogany chamber horse *Webb*
132 Six chairs, cane seats *Nicholls*
133 Deal dressing table and cover
134 Beautiful swing glass, mahogany frame, with marble slab, plate 24 in. by 18 in. *Wood*

135 Very handsom mahogany ft. by 2 ft.
136 Splendid mal robe, with drawers un 9 in., by 4 f
137 Carpet and ru
138 Rug
139 Mahogany cur massive rin curtains
140 Two roller bli

Chintz Ch

141 Set of capi half-tester b *Hall* chintz furnit pink cambri
142 Wool mattress
143 Excellent dow and 2 pillow
144 Pair of blanke
145 Large quilt
146 Wire fender, v and knobs
147 Set of fire iron
148 Chimney orna
149 Four chairs, ca
150 Mahogany nig
151 Deal dressing
152 Swing glass, m with 3 draw
153 Mahogany wa carved bacl
154 Neat toilet ser
155 Water bottle a
156 Double-rail ch
157 Mahogany wa slides & 3 d *Warner* neath, 7 ft.,
158 Carpet and ru
159 Piece of oilclot
160 Chintz wind lined with and mahoga
161 Roller blind

Green Chamber.

62 Set of handsome mahogany fluted four-post bedsteads, chintz furniture, lined with cambric, deep worsted fringe, and cornice
63 Flock mattress
64 Capital feather bed, bolster, and pillow
65 Pair of blankets
66 Wire fender, brass rim
67 Set of fire irons
68 Chimney ornaments
69 Oval pier glass
70 Large handsome mahogany chest of drawers, circular front
71 Mahogany couch, hair mattress, and pillow
72 Painted dressing chest, nine drawers
73 Mahogany wash stand, with marble top
74 Handsome china toilet service, 9 pieces
75 Water bottle and goblet
76 Double-rail chamber horse

177 Handsome swing glass, mahogany frame, plate 21 ins. by 15 ins.
178 Mahogany wardrobe, with 4 slides, 6 ft. 9 ins. by 4 ft.
179 Oval pier glass
180 Carpet to fit room, 15 ft. by 15 ft.
181 Rug to match
182 Two pieces of oilcloth
183 Mahogany curtain pole, rings and muslin curtain
184 Iron rod with green curtain
185 Two roller blinds

Dressing Room.

186 Ottoman
187 Painted wash stand
188 Blue and white toilet service 9 pieces
189 Water bottle and goblet
190 Chamber horse
191 Painted chest of drawers
192 Swing glass, mahogany frame
193 Backgammon board
194 Drugget
195 Two pieces of oilcloth
196 Roller blind

END OF THIRD DAY'S SALE.

FOURTH DAY'S SALE,

Thursday, Oct. 26, 1865,

COMMENCING AT 11 O'CLOCK.

Well-Harvested Hay.

In a Field adjoining Railway Station.

1 Rick of capital hay, growth 1864, (to go off) *Baffer*
2 Rick of capital hay, growth 1865, (to go off) *Hudson*

The hay will be sold in East Castle St.

Stable and Coach House.

3 Excellent dark bay carriage gelding, 6 years old, 15 hands 1 inch high, very fast in harness, and a capital hack
4 Well-built gig, in good condition, with lamps & cover *tw*
5 Capital 4-wheel carriage, lined with blue cloth, with pole, shafts, and lamps complete and cover to ditto *Horton*
6 Set of gig harness
7 Two gig collars *Edwards*
8 Saddle and bridle *Roberts*
9 Ditto *Sannatt*
10 Two head collars
11 Horse cloth and roller *Parsons*
12 Six brushes, comb, and wash leather
13 Pikel, broom, whisket, and rake *Matthews*
14 Corn bin
15 Carriage jack *Edwards*
16 Gas stove

Scullery.

17 Curtain rod and sundries
18 Two large oval iron pots
19 Tin fish kettle and drainer *val.*
20 Ditto *Parker*
21 Large tin turbot kettle *2s in Ko*
22 Three iron saucepans *Harding*
23 Three ditto *Hughes*
24 Three ditto *Matthews*
25 Two frying pans and gridiron *2s*
26 Four small pans *Edwards*
27 Four tins *2s*
28 Dutch oven, colander, tin bowl, and bucket *Brown*
29 Lemon squeezer, 2 gravy strainers, brush, soup ladle and 2 basting spoons *Mann*
30 Two chopping knives & block
31 Four sieves *Wright*
32 Bird cage and coal box
33 Meat block and cleaver
34 Three smoothing irons *Hughes*
35 Copper tea kettle *Wallford*
36 Ditto *Musgrave*
37 Ditto
38 Two tin buckets *Jones*
39 Paste slab and pin *Warner*
40 Fender and coffee pot *Edwards*
41 Long bench *Newall*
42 Oak claw table *Clive*
43 Small table, with drawer *nus*
44 Long deal table
45 Large plate rack

Kitchen.

Fender, tongs, and poker *warm*.
Five brass candlesticks *Son*
Brass mortar and pestle and cheese toaster *cele*
Four scollop shells *Warner*
Two boxes of paste cutters
Pair of snuffers and tray
Patent scales *Farmer*
Coffee and pepper mills
Pair of bellows and fork *Edwards*
Copper coal box *Simms*
Two ditto *Williams*
Copper warming pan *Noline*
Ditto *Wild*
Large brass kettle *Edwards*
Large maslin ditto *Wild*
Two copper stewpans *Wander*
Small ditto and brass pan
Tin tea kettle, bowl, and cheese toaster *Mansfield*
Tin hastener with brass bottle jack *Jacon*
Seven block tin dish covers *Warner*
Three copper moulds *Wander*
Wire wisk *Warner*
Pudding tins
Quantity of tin patties and paste cutters *Edwards*
Three brass taps
Metal tea pot & sugar nippers *Price*
Ditto ditto
White jug and 3 cups *Brown*
Odd tea cups and saucers
Quantity of white preserve pots *Warner*
Ditto glass ditto
Six cake tins *Brewster*
Quantity of blancmange moulds *Warner*
Spice box and tinware *Warner*
Quantity of preserves
Clothes horse *Wander*
Four ash chairs *Vaughan*
Deal table and cover

84 Deal dresser
85 Two hassocks and
.86 Capital 8-day cloc

Bacon.

87 Flitch of home-cur per lb.
88 Ditto ditto
(89 Ham of ditto, at)
(90 Ditto ditto

Landing

91 Capital linen pres
92 Stair carpeting, 1(
93 Twelve brass rods
94 Brussels carpet, to room, 17 ft. b
95 Rug to match
96 Capital large dru;
97 Two pieces of K: carpet
98 Piece of Brussels
99 Eighteen ft. of st;
100 Twenty-nine ft.
101 Piece of matting pieces of carpe
102 Stair carpet cove
103 Piece of oil clotl
104 Two mats

AFTERNOON

Commencing at 2

Chamber, 1

105 Set of painted tester bedst beautiful chin lined with car
106 Capital wool ma
107 Excellent feathe and pillow
108 Pair of blankets
109 Pair of ditto
110 Counterpane
111 Wire fender, wi and knobs

112 Set of fire irons
113 Hip bath
114 Three toilet cans
115 Set of half-tester bedsteads, with rich chintz furniture, lined with cambric
116 Mattress
117 Painted maple wash table
118 Toilet service, 11 pieces
119 Water bottle and goblet
120 Double-rail chamber horse
121 Three chairs, seg bottoms
122 Mahogany dressing chest, fitted with 7 drawers
123 Handsome swing glass, mahogany frame, plate 24 ins. by 18 ins
124 Handsome cabinet, fitted up with 12 drawers
125 Splendid model of Jerusalem and stand, by Edwin Smith, Sculptor and Modeller, Sheffield
126 Cover to ditto
127 Mahogany chest of drawers
128 Neat painted bookshelf
129 Drugget, 16 ft. by 15 ft., and rug to match
130 Piece of oil cloth and roller blind

Chamber, No. 2.

131 Set of mahogany fluted four-post bedsteads, with crimson moreen furniture
132 Hair mattress
133 Excellent feather bed, bolster, and 2 pillows
134 Pair of blankets
135 Pair of ditto
136 Wire fender with brass rim
137 Set of fire irons
138 Coal vase
139 Foot pan and hot water can
140 Painted wash stand
141 Toilet service, 7 pieces

142 Double-rail painted chamber horse
143 Small mahogany chest of drawers
144 Ditto, circular front
145 Mahogany dressing table, with drawer
146 Swing glass, mahogany frame
147 Mahogany Pembroke table
148 Five chairs, cane seats
149 Chimney glass, 3 ft. 9 ins. by 18 ins.
150 Drugget and rug
151 Piece of oilcloth and roller blind

Chamber, No. 3.

152 Set of half-tester bedsteads, with drab moreen furniture and straw mattress
153 Thick hair mattress
154 Capital feather bed, bolster, and 2 pillows
155 Pair of blankets
156 Coverlet
157 Chamber horse
158 Flower pot stand
159 Two chairs, cane seats
160 Two Uxbridge ditto
161 Small deal table and desk
162 Swing glass, mahogany frame
163 Ditto
164 Painted chest of drawers
165 Ditto
166 Painted washstand
167 Blue and white toilet service, 8 pieces
168 Painted dressing table
169 Mahogany ditto
170 Alarum
171 Mahogany corner wash-hand stand and ware
172 Four pieces of carpet
173 Dimity window curtains

Chamber, No. 4.

174 Set of half-tester bedsteads, with drab moreen furniture, and straw mattress
175 Flock mattress
176 Capital feather bed, 2 bolsters and 2 pillows
177 Pair of blankets
178 Pair of ditto
179 Chair and water can
180 Two Uxbridge chairs
181 Painted corner wash-hand stand
182 Blue and white ware

183 Painted corner wash stand
184 Blue and white ware
185 Small painted dressing table
186 Ditto
187 Swing glass, mahogany frame
188 Ditto
189 Painted chamber horse
190 Large painted maple chest of drawers
191 Three pieces of printed drugget
192 Chintz window curtains
193 Mahogany shoe rack

ROWLEY, PRINTER, HIGH STREET, BRIDGNORTH.